MCR

VERKLEMPT:
THE BOARD GAME

MR. LATKEHEAD

REUBEN'S
CUBE

JACOB-IN-THE-BOX

THE
OY-OY!

OY!

BONUS POINTS FOR
NOT RUNNING

THE OLD
'MENORAH-
THROUGH-THE-
HEAD' GAG!

JUN 07 2017

D1159252

Dedicated to my mom,
Esther (a.k.a. Christmas),
and to the memory of my dad,
Moe (a.k.a. Yom Kippur).

Text and illustrations copyright © 2016 (pending) by Mark Tuchman.
All rights reserved. No part of this book may be reproduced or transmitted
in any form without permission in writing from the author.

The illustrations were created with felt tip marker, and digitally
colored using Photoshop CS3 and a mouse. Yes, a mouse!

Special thanks to Michelle, Michael, Jennifer, Linda, Matthew, Brian,
Mahnaz, Gail, Larry, and my children (Sam, Lily and Ella).
And to the Tuchmans I grew up with, and their families.

Hanukkah With Uncle Reuben: Not Santa...but Not Bad
By Mark Tuchman
1st edition.
ISBN 978-0-9978948-1-3
Visit www.unclereuben.com

Hanukkah With Uncle REUBEN

NOT SANTA but Not Bad

By Mark Tuchman

All children love Santa.
Of this, there's no doubt.
But sadly, some homes
Are not on his route.

Bubeleh, don't worry.
There's someone for you.
His name's Uncle Reuben
And I promise, he'll do.

Long-time believers
Of kindly Saint Nick
May say Reuben copied
The jolly man's shtick.

He's no Santa rip-off.
That charge is unfair.

Each has his own style.
Let's contrast and compare.

Reuben lives on
The Lower East Side,

Santa's crystal ball shows
Who's naughty or nice.

Reuben learns this from
His friend Nora Weiss.

Santa fits every toy
In a sack on his sled.

Rubes has an old suitcase
Kept under his bed.

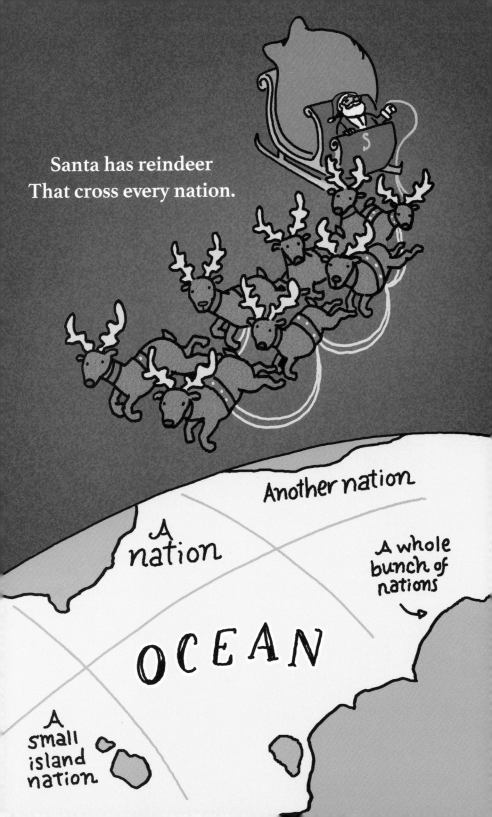

Santa has reindeer
That cross every nation.

Another nation

A nation

A whole bunch of nations

OCEAN

A small island nation

Reuben believes in
Public transportation.

Down the chimney goes Santa
With toys in a sack.

Reuben uses the door,
Hey, he's got a bad back.

Claus arrives when it's quiet.
That's not Reuben's deal.

He enjoys conversation
(And sometimes a good meal.)

Santa's toys are elf-made.
They're modern and glitzy,

Reuben has tchotchkes
He got from Aunt Mitzi.

Santa never lingers

But Reuben's just starting.

**He'll tell stories and jokes
Even sing before parting.**

Reuben's no youngster
And may sometimes request,

"I'm feeling quite winded.
Would you mind if I rest?"

You've heard Santa say

Uncle Reuben? He says

No sleigh or reindeer
Yet Reuben persists,

And goes to the house
That's next on his list.

Santa gets it all done,
Makes it seem like a breeze.

Reuben does what he can
But makes no guarantees!

Now some Jewish children
May prefer old Saint Nick.

Well I'm sorry you guys
But you don't get to pick.

ETCH-A
KVETCH

"YOU
KNOCKED
MY KIPPA OFF"
(GAME)

FUZZY DREIDELS

KASHA!

POTATO!

ASK the
ALL-KNOWING

BUNDLE
UP!

ZOLA

IT'S A
GARMENT CENTER
IN A TUB!

MUGS
FROM MOM